All My Important Nothings

edited by Maura Dooley

smith|doorstop

Published 2015 by
smith|doorstop Books
The Poetry Business
Bank Street Arts
32-40 Bank Street
Sheffield S1 2DS

ISBN 978-1-910367-42-1
Typeset by Utter
Printed by MPG Biddles

smith|doorstop Books are a member of Inpress:
www.inpressbooks.co.uk. Distributed by Central Books Ltd.,
99 Wallis Road, London E9 5LN

The Poetry Business gratefully acknowledges the support
of Arts Council England.

Contents

Dear Elizabeth Bennet

Dear Elizabeth Bennet, now you are old,
So far out of your youth that all of those
You knew then are dead or departed,
Even all your sisters, even lovely Jane;
At this point, and with the man gone too,
But him so taciturn in later years
That you do not miss him; at this juncture,
With so few years left – there can be no doubt
That even your robust health must fail, and no
Dances or taking of the waters here or there –
Might I, who suddenly finds himself similarly
Dispersed across time and without a fortune,
Might I be permitted to take your offered arm
And execute a slow turn around the grounds?

Emma, you're a gamer

'Seldom, very seldom, does complete truth belong to any human disclosure.'

Emma, you're a gamer. Backgammon, anagrams,
the matches and the banter.
     You're a natural. Serve and volley
back and forth in argument – the provocation, the resolve,
those little zigzags of embarrassment -
     one hundred different ways of being in love.

Emma, you're a dreamer. You're a strategist. a schemer –
the metagame of manners,
     all those formal misdemeanours,
the compliments, charades.
     Emma, you're a charmer.
You're a looper and a reeler. The surliest grammarian
would melt to see you dance.
     Emma, you're a gamer.
Who knows better than the dealer
the hazards and the chances, the advantage of a match,
the ricrac interlock of suit and fortune.

Oh Emma, it's a screamer. All the riddles, the enigmas –
the courtship in a sonnet,
     the conundrums on the hill.
Yes he's frank, but is he candid. Someone blundered,
someone's bluffing,
     and someone's slipped a joker in the pack.
The letters on the table rearranged to name your error –
Emma, you're a goner, don't you know you've met your match?

Emma, that's *amore*. So it goes, same old story –
the word you didn't know,

                                 the trick you had to miss.
The hint that every night has sat and stared you in the face
while you punted little sallies to and fro.

                                         Give it up now, little ego,
there's a prize for second place,
and Emma, you're an amateur, you're up against a pro.

The Bonnet

That Samhain we dressed as characters
        from *Persuasion:* we gender-bended
through the Finglas fields. I wore velvet
        trousers and cravat. You pranced about
in a bonnet nicknamed Jane Austen:
        golden straw sprigged with silk columbine.

By the time we sat summer exams
        you were wasted. We read in your eyes
the opened grave, the funeral rain.

White Knightley

If I loved you less, says
Knightley, *I might be able
to talk about it more. But
you know what I am ...*

a kind of writer, in fact,
who knows love can lie
in language more easily
than clean white sheets.

*At present, I ask only
to hear, once to hear
your voice...* in reality,
he asks the impossible.

Writers respect silence,
the two inches of ivory
untouched by a brush,
thirsty for their images.

It fills most of this page,
words forming squares
like infantry set against
Napoleon's white horse.

Writers' nights are white,
often fearing ivory gates,
or they wake white-eyed,
plucking at their sheets.

Jane Austen: Selected Letters

for my mother, Julia Ann

Then, each in its peculiar honours clad,
Shall publish even to the distant eye
Its family and tribe. Laburnum rich
In streaming gold
            – William Cowper, *The Task*, 1785

1

Where shall I begin? she starts. Which of all
my important nothings shall I tell you first?
In her shortened sign-off, above, she'd *remain*

with Love,
            Yrs affec JA.

I read names into that unwritten absence;
Julia Ann ... who helped shape my initial scribbles
and kept an old card with first words in my hand:

from Zaffar
            – the *ff* pointing backwards,

back to that consonant I couldn't then say;
stuck with my start, I was an Affer, or Faffer –
which proved true, Mum later said, of the latter.
Dawdler that I became. So here I am

taken aback by letters – their afterlife –
and how we draw together when they arrive.

2

We also talk of a Laburnam. – The Border
under the Terrace Wall is clearing away ...

I go back and look at her misplaced *a*
in *Laburnam*. It's you, Mum, I remember
explaining to me how a soft Indian u
is equally an a. My dad taught me to say
'Mera nam Zaffar hai'. The first vowel
in my name like the last u in laburnum.

As a child I'd climb that tree, spend hours lost in
its grey-green limbs at the end of our garden.

Early days, at the registry, in Birmingham
Mum wrote out, in her own spelling ... *Kunial*;
from Jat-Rajput-Kanyal – Dad's tribe or clan,
starting past those parts that talk of caste.

In Austen

that *A*, almost from the off, is a different sound –
more like the o in of, than the u in ground.

A Swansea Education (1977)

CHORE
S'RUNNER
PRAYER
LEWDER
NUTH
AIR
LOW
ENÉMA

– SAUL
RE:
JUNCYING
LONDON
CAW
MICK
EYE
RUNNY

MARCH
MAY
KINNUN
INN
TOUGH
EARRING
HONOUR
NON

– SARDLY
AIR
RICK
MAW
CUM
HORREUR
KNEE
WHYS!

RUE
R.P.
MISS
TONIGHT
LEIGH?
RUE
R.P.
NOW?

ISS
LIE
FIZZ
ARE
DINUFF
WEAR
NITS
O.K.

Costume Drama

And now it was Mum's turn
to ask the questions:
why was I showing so much leg,
why was I wearing lip gloss,
why was I going for a walk,
why wouldn't I watch Jane Austen?

If I'd have known the answers,
I'd have been unhappier than I was
after church, after polishing
my parents' silver, after the belly
of pork, after hearing my step-father
regurgitate *The News of the World*.

That afternoon, I was followed
by a short man in a brown leather jacket,
Polaroids and moustache.
I hurried on, crossed the road,
ducked into the garden of the bungalow
next to the library, jabbed at the bell, heart

chipping the enamel of my teeth.
They wouldn't let me in.
I explained. Pointed. Turned.
The man had gone.
They shut the door, went back
to the crinoline of Sunday afternoons.

I ran the five minutes home,
burst in on *Persuasion.*
In the kitchen, in the adverts,
Mum sympathised but wasn't surprised:
why was I wearing such a short dress,
why had I wanted to go out, anyway?

I will not say that your mulberry trees are dead; but I am afraid they're not alive

He was passing up the hill and within a few yards of her
when her accident happened.
He was carrying a gun. The whole country about them
abounded in beautiful walks.

He apologized for his intrusion by relating its cause.
He meant to offer some kind of explanation.

He would not stop to expatiate on the absurdity
but threatened her with rain.

The Clouds United Over Their Heads.

'You will begin to think I am never worth going
through the rain for'. She warned him.

He coloured and stammered out an unintelligible reply.

He was passing up the hill and within a few
yards of her when her accident happened but
I cannot speak well enough to be unintelligible.

Aunties

Other Aunties they are long married
with two-two children. This Auntie
however did not find any good boy, or found
and let him slide out of her hands,
but sometimes, you understand, these things
are for the best. No man will be happy
dangling for dinner, waiting waiting while wife
is occupying all day with hobbies, sewing sewing,
writing writing, hiding hiding, showing
no-one. Still she is fully functioning, doing
fine needlework, see see this bag, this small
crochet, such a sharp eye she has in spite of age.
Sharp tongue also. Always I say, 'Auntie,
you are making me laugh only with wicked mimic
of next-door Mrs Banot, how she is always
spinning spinning, lying in spiderwait
to catch the flies for those five girls. Poor
things, marriageable still but almost
past sell-by, well on the way
to being like you,
before they know it,
Aunties too'.

Jane and Juan

> *'I wonder who first discovered the efficacy of poetry in driving away love! ...*
> *I am convinced that one good sonnet will starve it entirely away.'*
> — *Pride and Prejudice*, Chapter 9, 1813

> *'When amatory poets sing their loves*
>   *In liquid lines mellifluously bland,*
> *And pair their rhymes as Venus yokes her doves,*
>   *They little think what mischief is in hand.'*
> — *Don Juan*, Canto 5, 1820

Slipped under her door at midnight, the sonnet
Didn't hold back. Eyes, ears, mouth, bosom, lips:
'Such beauty as yours can never be eclipsed.'
I even praised the way she wore her bonnet.

At breakfast, the chambermaid passed a note.
'I'm in debt to your kind words, which my heart tells
Me would be better bestowed on someone else,
If they've not been already. Yours, E Bennet.'

How to get such a woman into bed?
I used to score with the flimsiest stuff.
Now her kind are worse than critics. When I tried
Her again just now with my most tested love
Song, she cut off my recital midway and cried
'Stop – you have delighted me long enough.'

'The mere habit of learning to love is the thing.'
(Northanger Abbey)

Begin small:
not the extravagance of sunsets
or that expensive tender sirloin.

Notice the wobbly heart
marked on a grey pebble
or a forgotten conker sprouting.

Keep at it:
Order mussels; shells like cupped palms
offering me a gift I'd thought I wouldn't like.

The habit of loving
is hard to learn. We think
we know how and say we do.

Today a February sun backlights
two pigeons perched side-by-side,
iridescent, ready to start again.

Northanger Abbey

for Catherine rising regular in the stirrups and the long-coated
horsemen with whips and the stopping to change for a phaeton,
for Catherine lurking

in a cabinet of yellow Japan, for Catherine's long-gallery
longings of fictive lives masquerading the fancy of a fabulous
murder by a general,

for Catherine of the gargoyles and sugar plums and teapot tastes
of Staffordshire clay, for Catherine of the silk tambour gown
and soft silhouettes,

for Catherine swearing off praise for she's never by halves,
for the grand clock and Catherine parading in the Pump Room
for the full-five

minute suspense sitting still midst the coxcombs and coquettes
when Catherine's not taken for cotillions, for Catherine going
Psha!

for a man at the elbow and the humbling to dust, the parting
promises of the fair ones, for Catherine learning to love
a hyacinth,

for coming up from a low in the valley with its wood oaks,
for Catherine the heroine of the three thousand pounds,
whose parents give

a fig for the suasions of her heart, for Catherine under covers
and the fire already roaring for the glad show, the dreamboat
without plunge or caper

defying his father to dance his Catherine at a country dance!

A Visitor

I am toothless, white haired, twenty one.

I was fifteen, though no one counted the years,
but me. I hid in the corn like a deer.
When I raised my head to see,
the press gang pounced and netted me.

At the end, I lay on the stilled deck.
Under my eyelids, fiery ships flashed.
Scorched hands stuck to broken timbers.
For days, I was a log that no one could flog
into obedience. At last, the captain set me loose,
a dog limping homewards.

Now the door creaks, as I push my way in.
My tongue can't find the words I want.
Bread. A slice of ham. All that comes:
a toothless flip-flap of lips, a dying fish.

I watch the marvel of clean muslin arms
and the little curl escaping from her cap.
Her pen drifts over small inky sheets.
She scissors out islands of script.
Captain Benwick, Captain Wentworth, Admiral Croft.
She takes long pins and tacks the new words
over old sentences. I gather the cut paper,
squinny at her through its holes.

I could stop your ears with my story, I say.

She stares me out through the paper mask.
I hear her sigh. *I can't write what I don't know.*
There's an apple pie in the kitchen. Eat it, please.
Then, I must let you go.

At Chawton

In her room in the quiet house
her small table is a saucer
where her quick pen dips, her mind
in conversation with the world.

In the garden, flowers open their throats
to the rummage of bees, till dusk darkens
the page, and a last rush of starlings
scrawls its closing sentence on the sky.

In a hundred years, a hundred more,
a girl reading at a table laps the words
of every elegant line, each turned
page an opening door.

Reader, desire is the dark avenue
to Pemberley. You hardly breathe,
imagining the dance, a light hand laid
between your shoulder-blades.

Towards a Diagnosis

Think of your body as a room containing *neither tapestry nor velvet*,
a room not as capacious as first thought.
Something large and unexpected has appeared
half shoved into an alcove it is too big for.
What can it hold? Why should it be placed here?
Its handles have been broken *by some strange violence*
and on its lid is *a mysterious cypher*:
Wrenched, unreadable and out of place,
it demands all your strength to raise its lid.
Inside is a single practical item, colourless and *properly folded*.
You step back and laugh at yourself in the growing dark.
Raising your candle, you only then notice
the other thing there across the room. So much less obvious
but entrancingly foreign in its surfaces. The key is in the lock.
You try different angles, pressures and rotations
telling yourself all the while that you have only *the smallest
expectation of finding anything,* tipping what's left of your candle,
your eyes *quite tired of dust and lamps.* When it gives
and the door flies open, you've no idea how it was done.
Small drawers and larger drawers and at their centre
a tiny door with a key. First the drawers:
each was equally empty. There remains the door.
It would be foolish not to examine it.
Once again you discover the particular
pressure or angle which you instantly forget.
You reach in and touch a scroll of paper
which you hold to your candle just as its flame goes out.
I have had a good deal of fever at times and indifferent nights.
You lie there in the roar of the storm.
The paper on the floor.
At first light you read its list of facts.

Persuasion

for Julia Darling

In the car in Cape Town – suddenly you were there
Surprisingly clear in the suburbs of Newlands.
You whispered to Bev Rycroft and me, from the back seat,
Tapped us on the shoulder, you said two words
As if all language had left was this: Two Lighthouses.
Across the parting of the tide, apartheid, the Atlantic Ocean,
Over Table Bay, Bantry Bay, Bakoven, Table Mountain,
You'd passed the ghost of Mandela on Robben Island.
As if time could stand still and still move forward.
As if all at sea would not be lost – as if the dead could
Light the lighthouse light to guide the living.

Then it seems not long ago now when you were leaving
Newcastle, the Tyne weaving, the house in the Vale,
Your friends, your lover, your two daughters. Already
Far away from the house where you were born in Winchester,
Where Jane Austen spent the last weeks of her life, died.
You remember the faces at the window looking for Jane.
Perhaps Jane tapped your shoulder, tired of landed gentry,
Told you to tell the truth about mastectomies, hot flushes.
Perhaps women writers pass the baton, nod, affirm, across seas,
Prides, prejudices, races, classes, senses, sensibilities.
You said it; we heard it, clear as Grace. Two Lighthouses.

About the authors

Gillian Clarke has published fourteen collections of poems. Her work is studied by GCSE and A Level students throughout Britain. She was founder and is President of Ty Newydd writers' centre in North Wales. The Welsh landscape is a shaping force in her work, together with recurrent themes of war, womanhood and the passage of time. In 2010 she was awarded the Queens Gold Medal for Poetry.

Jonathan Davidson grew up in Didcot and has lived for many years in Coventry. He has published three collections of poetry, three pamphlets and had eight radio plays broadcast on BBC Radio 3 and 4, along with radio adaptations of Geoffrey Hill's *Mercian Hymns* and W.S.Graham's *The Nightfishing*. He won an Eric Gregory Award and is a poetry-theatre producer. His most recent touring shows were *Being Human* (2012/13) and *The Hundred Years' War* (2015/16).

Imtiaz Dharker, poet, artist and documentary film-maker, was born in Pakistan, grew up in Scotland and lived for many years in India. She was awarded the Queen's Gold Medal for Poetry in 2014, is a recipient of the Cholmondeley Award and a Fellow of the Royal Society of Literature. Travelling with a caravan of poets on Poetry Live! she reads to over 25,000 students a year.

Maura Dooley has published four collections of poetry and is a Fellow of the Royal Society of Literature. *The Silvering*, new poems, will be published in 2016. From 2014-15 she was Poet-in-Residence at the Jane Austen House Museum, Chawton. Her poems from the residency are published as a sister-pamphlet: *A Quire of Paper*.

Ian Duhig has won the Forward Best Poem Prize, the National Poetry Competition twice and three times been shortlisted for the T S Eliot Award. His seventh collection of poetry, *The Blind Roadmaker* will be published by Picador in February 2016.

Lavinia Greenlaw has published novels, criticism and memoir as well as five collections of poetry including *Minsk*, which was shortlisted for the T.S. Eliot, Forward and Whitbread Poetry Prizes. Her most recent book *A Double Sorrow: Troilus and Criseyde* was shortlisted for the Costa Poetry Award.

Jackie Kay is an award-winning writer of fiction, poetry and plays. She has published five collections of poetry for adults (*The Adoption Papers* won the Forward Prize, a Saltire Award and a Scottish Arts Council Book Award) and several for children. She was awarded an MBE in 2006.

Stephen Knight was born in Swansea. He worked as a theatre director, then as a tutor in creative writing firstly for the University of Glamorgan, later at Goldsmiths, London University. He won an Eric Gregory Award as well as the National Poetry Competition and has published three collections most recently, *The Prince of Wails* (2012). He has also published a novel and a collection of poems for children: *Sardines*.

Zaffar Kunial's first collection of verse was published as part of the Faber New Poets series in 2014. Much of his work to date has drawn creatively on his rich cultural inheritance as an Anglo-Asian writer, and what he calls the "the legacy of exchanging words across the centuries." In 2014 he was Poet-in-Residence at the Wordsworth Trust.

Paula Meehan was born and lives in Dublin. As well as her poetry she has written plays and conducted writing workshops with inner city communities, in prisons, schools and universities. Her work is much translated, widely anthologized, and among the prizes she has won are The Martin Toonder Award , the Butler Literary Award and the Denis Devlin Award . She is a member of Aosdána, and is Ireland Professor of Poetry, 2013 – 2016.

Blake Morrison was born in Yorkshire. He has written plays, poetry, novels, libretti and literary criticism. His non-fiction includes the memoirs *And When Did You Last See Your Father?* and *Things My Mother Never Told Me*. His most recent poetry collection, *Silver Street*, was published in 2015. He is Professor of Creative Writing at Goldsmiths, London.

Daljit Nagra won two categories in the Forward Prize for his first collection of poetry and also for its title poem, 'Look, We Have Coming to Dover!'. His second book, was chosen by *The Guardian* and *The Independent* as 'poetry book of the year'. Nagra has recently published a new version of the *Ramayana: a Retelling*. Born in Middlesex, he lives in London, where he works as an English teacher.

Katrina Naomi is a poet and tutor. Her latest publication is *Hooligans*, a pamphlet inspired by the Suffragettes. Her new collection *The Way the Crocodile Taught Me* will be published by Seren in 2016. She is a lecturer at Falmouth University, runs Poetry Surgeries for the Poetry Society and is a 2015 Hawthornden Fellow.

Stephanie Norgate is a playwright and poet, who grew up in Selborne, close to Chawton and grew up reading Gilbert White and Jane Austen. Her pamphlet *Fireclay* was published by smith|doorstop books and was followed by *Hidden River* (Bloodaxe, 2008), shortlisted for the Forward First Collection Prize and the Jerwood Aldeburgh Prize and *The Blue Den* (Bloodaxe, 2012). She edited *Poetry and Voice*, a collection of essays (Cambridge Scholars Publishing, 2012). She is Reader in Creative Writing at the University of Chichester.

Abigail Parry wrote her doctoral thesis on poetry and play. She is currently Writer in Residence at the National Videogames Arcade.

Alicia Stubbersfield's fourth poetry collection *The Yellow Table* was published in 2013. She lectured in Creative Writing at The University of Aberystwyth and Liverpool John Moores University. A regular tutor for The Arvon Foundation, Alicia is currently Writer-in-Residence for a Schools Project organised by Cheltenham Festivals and First Story.

Jack Underwood was one of the first four poets as part of the Faber New Poets pamphlets scheme in 2009. He is a Lecturer in English and Creative Writing at Goldsmiths College, tutor at the Poetry School, reviewer for *Poetry London* and *Poetry Review*, and founding editor, with Sam Riviere of *Stop/Sharpening/Your/Knives*. His debut collection, Happiness, was published in 2015.